idiot

parade

GOTT PRESS

"Trash" was originally published by Literally Literary on Medium in August 2017 and "Hate Machines" by Rad Press in Issue 2 of The Cult, November 2017.

www.gabegott.com
www.gottpress.com

$10.00
ISBN 978-0-692-09359-7
51000>

9 780692 093597

Thank you Akron Soul Train
for making this possible.

To artists everywhere. The world needs us.

Table of Contents

unbroken

for a   flash of time
        half shrouded
                        leaping,   from a preci-
pice

            the   harpoons
                            scattered   the
expressions of   fright

the barnacled flank

in the great bowels below
                                        carries   his
t   o   d
    a

                            raging
in   art
            of   a
        li   o   e

tutored by

living and breathing

he cared about

be   ing

famous,

rarely
w   i   th

integrity

The

De
v   i   l

Apprentice   s

say yes to
h   I   s

power.

Martyrs

you say, "sweet dreams,"
but mine are terrifying
if I said I wasn't scared
you'd know
I would be lying

when I wake up
my dreams wake up with me
and maybe I've never
really been asleep
and this is
all just a
waking
night
mare

walking down
the street
distrust glowing
in everyone's eyes
tension in the air:
colorless, odorless,
but we all
know it's there

like nitroglycerin,
it's only a matter
of time before
it goes
and the air
explodes,
swarming
hornets around
the offender
who said just
the wrong thing
or maybe made
a funny
face

high and
mighty
on our throne
of thrones
our judgment
final with a
growing list
of what we don't
condone

we are our own
evangelists

and everything we
do is righteous
in our
minds,
no matter what,
it can be
justified

if we took
a moment,
if we made the
time, we
would see
that to which
we've
become
willfully
blind

the world is
crumbling
around us &
society is
in flames
we are fooling
no one,
multiplying

shames

let's be
realistic
we have
never been
more
lost &
we are
going nowhere
nailed upon
the cross

but we
are not
Jesus
we
aren't
even the
thieves
we
nailed
our-
selves
to it
just
to

feel
the
ble-
ed

Expectations

Expectations rule the day
Can't get out of their way
Tell you what to think
And what to say

Marching up and down the street
Strictly marching to the beat
Marching hard and marching right
Marching in your head in the dead of night

What can you do but
Find the beat
And march beside them
In the street?

If it was that
Easy for everyone
There'd be no
One left
Staring into the sun
No one to
Watch the
Idiot parade

Exhaustion

The fog drifts,
mystifying the
landscape
absorbing the
sunlight
filtering
the glow to
shades of
grey

Thoughts meander
lazily,
boulders barely
floating,
damming
up down stream
the steel
blue gurgling
out,
absorbed
greedily
by the
dusty
earth
which
sputters
hoarsely
begging for more

The fog lifts
leaving the
sun to
beat down
angrily
making up
for lost time,
my vision
in flashing
color blotches,
the landscape
drowning deep in
shadows stealing
life
with
the
invisible teeth
of a tick

Unable
to flush
the pangs
of this
lusterless
radiation,
still I'm frozen,
stuck in place,
hunkered down
for the remains
of a dull day

1000110 1010101 1000011 1001011 1000101 1000100

ones and zeroes,
signals through
electronic pulses
creating
tiny dots
that make up
words and
pictures

we sit and
stare
at the screen
bombarded
by bits,
bitten by a
data addiction
thirsty for these
tiny ecstatic
moments
that keep us
hooked
through the
long spaces
of monotony

from which
we can't
draw away
even though
somewhere in
the back of our
brains we know
we should
but it's already
too late
we're already
too enmeshed—
insects drawn to a
bug zapper

Stewards of the Earth

The planet is not your garbage dump
it's not a place to dispose of the
things that don't biodegrade
maybe more stuff should be made to last
or at least reused &
if it's so easily trashed,
do we really need it?

The ocean does not need any floating
islands of plastic
the atmosphere doesn't need any extra
chemicals
the soil doesn't need any radioactive waste
or landfills—
the Earth is not your ash tray

You're not a very good steward
if you leave it worse than you found it,
if you let species die out
because of carelessness and greed
ignore the politics of climate change—
the talking points and word grenades
hurdled at people who don't
think the same

Find a remote place
one of the few that still exists
no noise pollution,
nothing man made,
no traffic, no factories,
no voices shouting
climb a mountain
to the highest peak
hike to the deepest
forest canopy
swim to the bottom
of the sea
find a place
the internet
doesn't
connect,
there's no
phone
service
or even
electricity
and
just take
it all in—
all the sights,
all the sounds,
everything

around,
and
ask
yourself
if you
really
deserve
any of
it

Cancer

When you have
cancer
You know the
answer

You shrink it
& medicate it
You cut it out
& radiate it

You don't just
leave it go
and let it grow
until it consumes
you

our poor brains beat

this old skull cracks

How the wild winds blow it
the torn shreds of split sails lash

prison corridors

come
tainted
a wicked, miserable world

b

y

naked men

most

steadfast,

swerve about, uncertain

unchangeable.

to   the

last

I am a selfish person

replete with examples of

financial gain

a business entrepreneur

plagued by the disease
of

profit

Disclaimer

a lie

a void
behind
a tie

Big
Brother
on the
wall

a voice
behind
a stall

walls
without a
mark

whispers
in the
dark

The Men of Ill-Repute

see the men of ill-repute
pandering pleasantries
in business suits
starched colors &
silken ties
vikings in a
gentleman
disguise

it's not insane
to do anything
to ease the pains
of capital gains

living high
has its
costs
no fortune
can be
lost

keep the masses
in line
swastikas
replaced
with dollar
signs

obedience-pledged

proletariat
slaves
to their debt
bleed to fulfill
their basic needs,
sell their potential
for some peace
of mind
keeping the faith
with the promise
of profit

but nothing
ever seems
to change
because
it wasn't
designed
that way—
there's
no profit
for those
with a
conscience
so
lose your
morals and
buy a suit,
and join the
men of
ill-repute

Narcissists

walking through time
with a rose held
to your nose
wearing
coats of arms
then cod pieces
and powdered wigs,
top hats through the
gilded age and
tuxedos in the
twenties,
you've always
been
fashion
able

through
the ages
you strut
and swagger
never afraid
to be the
braggart

holier than
thou art
You know
you are
so smart

because
you've
been
winning
since the
beginning
in a game
with no
shame

it's all
the same

as you
peer
into the
mirror
it could
n't be
clear
er

Opinions are like Assholes

you create a moment
just to counter
another moment
but it backfires
and they
both just
explode

What's your point of view,
tell me what it is,
What's it to you,
tell me what it
means...

We all might
Be sinners—
You tell it to
our face,
Through your
screed
On the screen
But I don't see
No saints

shout your words
as you
write them down—
make them loud

too proud to
save your kids, just
see us off and
watch us
drown
—finally,
that'll
show us
how

life's a fight
and
only the vicious
and the lucky
survive
the
night

v●id

thus,
wrapped up
in the flag
with
some rounds
in his mag
yankee doodle
went to town
and shot a few
people
down

hail victory
is what
he said
as the
crown
was placed
on his
head

hiding
behind
uncle sam
who shouted out
his commands
the generals
went about
their way

making plans
day after
day

see
the crowds
gather 'round
hear their boots
on the ground
marching
towards
the mire to
join their
voices
in the
choir

but
there's no
city on the hill
ruins razed
to rubble
strewn
beneath
the landfill

if what
fromm
said
is true
what is

there
to do?

we're
falling
away
further
each and
every day
into that
which
we can't
avoid
directly
into

the void

talk about power, money, and sex.

Those things   are
important to your success

                    w   n
                      he

you're desperately   empty, and
                            lying in   bed with
                                          millions of dollars
                              you

imagine

        everybody is wanting to be around you
t   o

                                          tell   you

how good you are

What death-knell rings

Keep him nailed-

-hoist the royals higher

In Jesus' name   this,
devil's madness

w   e Shall   keep chas-

ing

to the bottom of the sea

this   w   a   s

Ahab s
immutably decree
before   the Fates

cut down   the
lonely foo

l

The Glass is Empty

We're living in
dangerous
times
and everyone's
losing their
minds
but these
dangerous times
are by
intelligent
design

Cutting
down
the safety
nets
trading lives
to make bets
the stock market
is their
game
blood and money
are the
same

These
corporatist
leeches
they're
Star-bellied
Sneetches
and they
own
Mr McBean
so the split
grows
more obscene

We're more
desperate
by the day
trying not to
fade away
but taking home
less and less
hard to judge
our success

Hate Machines

boot steps echo,
stomping
across
concrete
torches darkening
deep shadows
on the wall
of America's
night

mob mentality
razing reason
voices shouting
rants & raves

hardened to hate
blaming brothers
and sisters for
plutocrats crimes,
convinced
differences
make us different
but we're
all the
same,
just
trying
to survive

the marchers
refuse to
empathize
feeding
the hate
machines,
driving each
other
to points
of no
return

By Any Other Name

just call it
what it is
when
you steal our
wealth and
leave us
in a ditch

the only thing
that trickles
down is when
you have
us held to
the ground
and all
we can
do is bite
our lip
with
a boot
to our
neck

when
you walk
away
feeling
relieved
you leave

our life
a wreck;
we'll try
to pick up
the pieces
but there's
not many
left

you're no
Robin Hood
robbing from
the poor
you're
nothing
but Prince
John's
whore

we're
on
a ledge
and you're
better off
with us
closer to
the edge

you push
harder
the more

we falter;
getting
giddy
with a
sacrifice
on your
altar

Babble

throw around
these words
like you know
what they mean
but it all
comes out
a jigsaw
puzzle
of escaping
steam

robbed of
vitality
detached from

reality

the speaker
has lost
touch
with
its
mean-
ing

all ideals
are incited
keeping us
divided
rumors on
bathroom
walls
trophies
tarnished
in the
hall
let us
out
of the
stocks
and
step
down
from
your
soap
box

if facts
are only
true
when

they
come
from you
ignorance
breeds
success
without
freedom
of the
press

stop
selling
our souls
to the
bigots
and the
fools
pack
up your
pulpit
enough
with
that
bullshit
set the
world

free
from
your
nega-
tivity

Trash

an empty coke can
on the side of the road
just waiting to get
crushed

the black earth
rattles as traffic speeds
past

the can
shudders
ever closer to
its fate

The end
No less
Savage than
The rest

terrif y

t h e

Ma
s
s es

—ask yourself this

question:
history even

good

for

busi-

ness

Socrates   said

start every day with a clean slate
open   our mind

of

architects

no one

learn t o   apply it.

the White Whale

diving down   disap-

peared

little Flask
twitching his legs
was lustily sing-

ing

—admitted of

a thousand   perils. -Ahab's

broad forehead

struck the surface

a stray oar,
touched his skin

as   h   e

continued his leeward

way

inextricable

fallen

Loneliness

Loneliness
is an astronaut floating in space
trying to save his oxygen
but drifting further away

watching the large blue ball
slowly spinning around
as he tumbles every which way
without an up or down

Maybe they'll send a shuttle
and there'll be a rescue
But maybe gravity will get him
and he'll burn up on return

most likely, though,
he'll just run out of air

And there he'll be floating
just another piece of debris
Some chunk of
space junk

For something like eternity

Document (15)

Out of body, out of mind
Nothingness personified

Stumbling in the dark,
haunted by horrors
No frame of reference
to latch onto
Invisible monsters
lurking around me
Reaching to get a grip
but catching only air

Feeling the shudder
Of another walking
over my grave
I try to make my way
But direction has
no meaning

Melancholy

Melancholy seeps into
the day, already
Well-worn

Color fades
Under the white
Light-trapped
Sky
Spilling
Tears of
Winter's
Slow death

Premature
flowers
wither
and wilt

Song birds
sing
of better
days
and fret
with grave
mistakes but
maybe they'll
find a way to
be born into a
new day

(If that day
should come
At last
And kill off
Winter's wrath,
the Earth still
on its tilt
toward
the sun,
a slow dive,
moment
by
moment
closer to
oblivion)

the colors
returning
at last,
melancholy
fading to an
afterthought

Celebrity Cake Walk

Everyone's a critic
A superhero social cynic
Join the parade
And let your mind
Be made

It's time to save
the day
All the good kids
Want to play

Take your
Moment and make
It your best
Put your head
Above the rest
Wait a second
And take a breath
Don't get queasy
It won't be easy

Step one foot
In the sanitarium
Get comfortable
And let yourself

Grow numb

Pull up a chair
All your
Favorite
Friends
Will be there
Just show them
What you're
About and
They'll never
Let you out

You'll spend
your days
In a daze—
It's what you
Wanted
Anyways

shocking to

fools

      faces;   man, in the ideal,
sparkling,

     blemish
their costliest   immaculate
selves,

           against the

        in

           dignity

omnipresence

               cast

       all,

ethereal light   I

forth   hyperspatial   hence-

do

n't shout   a t

the

the
maniac.

ge   on   ip

A   t f

a   g b   a

cup

a nd   b

e

r   e

b

orn.

Pride

I am a flawed
Human being,
Tempered by my flaws,
By acknowledging them
As intimate
Company
But not
Letting them
Define me

When I've got
Something to say,
I say it freely
But with restraint
Words more
Palpable when
Not shouted
But spoken
Out loudly

Pride is not
Necessarily
Negative
Especially when
It's righteous

(But not
Self-righteous)
Just because
I'm proud it
Doesn't mean
I think
I am always
Right

We might
Disagree,
But let's
Agree to
Disagree &
Try to
Coexist,
Harmoniously

Melodies have
Their counters,
Rhythms have their
Rhymes, just
Keep the beat
Steady, one
Beat at a
Time

Society is a
Symphony,
And we all
Have our
Parts to
Play

pigfuckers

Toast your cheese
and break up that
moldy bread
tell me what you
want, baby, and
you'll be handfed

Trade that grape
Kool Aid for a goblet
of wine
Let me reassure you
Everything will
be fine

Just keep both feet
planted
on the ground
Let love
into your
heart
and
don't let
those
damn dirty
pigfuckers
break you
down

Weathering

I feel it in my bones—

My mind wisps
windily,
cigarette smoke
splattered
by sprays of
cold
shower

Standing on the porch
trying to tackle
a hangover
to the cigarette's
expiration
before I
melt back into
the day...

Sprawling words
about a page
lines of inspiration—
a reverse rain dance

Maybe

Maybe I'm a lost cause
Maybe I'm a wanderer
Maybe I've got no home
but where I set my feet
Maybe
I'm just another
hobo on a train
Trying on different
facades
that flash past,
a moving picture
out my window
to the world

When I close
my eyes
I immerse
myself inside
them,
teleporting
to a new horizon
across a
fold in
space-time
in my mind

Embark

Kiss the piper
not the pauper
Always pay
the porter

Conspiracy
hoarders
talk out of order
balking about
the new
world
order

Flex your mind
like your forceps
Fuck the martyrs
embark
on a
new
mindset

The New Frontier

Blanketed by blackness
under the
star-speckled sky
the freshness of the
new day
fills my
lungs as
my footsteps
crunch against
the dirt,
direction
forming
as I
forge
ahead—
no road,
no trail,
nothing but
the new
frontier